ADRIFT IN A MIND

Stephen Murphy

Adrift in a Mind

Stephen Murphy was born in Rinteln, West Germany in 1968. He joined the Royal Navy at the age of 18 in 1987. He lives in Bedfordshire with his wife and two sons. *Adrift in a Mind* is his first collection of poems published in 2011.

First published in Great Britain in 2011

Copyright © Stephen Murphy, 2011

The right of Stephen Murphy to be identified as the author of this work has been asserted in accordance with Section 77 of the Copyright, Designs and Patent Act 1988

ISBN 978-1-61364-042-5

For Jack and Sam, and their Nanny Mary, my late Mum.

Contents

Acknowledgements

I would like to thank my wife Fiona for helping me name some of the poems in this book, I was able to write them but too often could not imagine their titles: without her there would have been a lot of "Untitled" poems.

I would also like to thank Norman Ross and Ruth Grimsley for giving me the faith and confidence to proceed with my dream of publishing a book of poems.

Adrift in a Mind

Christinaki

February,
1994,
February third,
to be precise.

Christinaki,
sank,
all crew,
lost at sea.

Herald steamed,
we tried to help,
we, like others,

too far away,
when, the mayday,
call, came.

You don't, mess,
with the sea.
I only saw, we only saw,

orange,
lifejackets, survival suits,
Rigid, Inflatable, Boats.

We, fought, the seas,
the battering we got,
we'd endured, before.

But everyone of us,
every man, beside,
every man, fell silent, that day.

I don't believe,
anyone survived,
the sinking,
of the Christinaki.

Eternal Ebb and Flow

Hand in hand, along the shingle beach,
Not another soul, ahead or behind,
The two of us walk, alone, hand in hand,
Walking alone on the everchanging shingle.

Each flow, picks up, a myriad of pieces,
Of that shingle, everchanging,
Each ebb replaces, new shape assumed,
Walking alone on the everchanging shingle.

New shape assumed, a million times over,
Minute on minute, year on year,
The spectrum of possibilities, never exhausted,
Walking alone on the everchanging shingle.

Generation on generation, the ebb and the flow,
Never ceasing to assume a new shape,
Time after time, minute after minute,
Walking alone on the everchanging shingle.

Since time immemorial, or so we're told,
Each flow picking up, each ebb replacing,
Like the good times, and the bad times,
Walking alone on the everchanging shingle.

Wind comes and goes and leaves, come and go,
There's nothing eternal, like the ebb and the flow,
Nothing so constant and nothing so sure,
Walking alone on the everchanging shingle.

Neptune's Wrath

You'll die a nasty death (spitting and gargling)
Of the sea, be thrown o'erboard and taken down.
The crashing, breaking, churning, sea of salt,
No aide, no rescue, no Neptune's crown,

Will save you from the danger of the sea,
If you don't heed the warning,
Batten down the hatches, stow away,
First and last, middle and morning.

Use the lanyards, buckles, stow for sea,
As swells increase, heave-to against,
The peaks and troughs, the breaking waves,
They don't recede once commenced.

Thousands of miles the swell does build,
Heave-to, full steam, whatever you must,
Like the fiercest tiger hot on heals,
Runaway, avoid the beast, at all cost.

Adrift in a Mind

Like walls of a cathedral,
Tree lined paths of mulch,
Of autumn leaves that have dropped,
From their dwelling,
Their life endorser.

Wandering through trees,
A mind that wanders,
From cathedral lined mulchpath,
To seas mirror calm,
Adrift in a mind.

Takes just a moment,
An image imagined,
To places once been,
And places once loved,
Places and times, spent wondering.

On the wide open seas,
A sea mirror calm,
Lands of nirvana, lands of utopia,
Behind, and ahead,
Adrift in a mind.

Alone up on deck, early, so early,
Not a word, not a noise,
From another to be heard,
Peace and serenity absorbed,
Places and times, spent wondering.

Back, and forth along lines,
Lines to be worked and surveyed,
For maps and charts and mariners alike,
Hour upon hour, day upon day,
Adrift in a mind.

From South Atlantic paths,
Being worked, mind drifting,
To tree lined cathedrals,
Cathedral lined mulchpath,
Places and times, spent wondering.

Adrift in a mind,
Places worlds apart,
Adrift in a mind,
Nirvana, Utopia all,
Adrift in a mind.

Impressionable Ages

I made a promise, a promise, to you both,
I looked into your eyes, at your soft, soft skin,
A promise for life, a promise to be kept,
So proud I looked at you both.

With fear, a thought, it came to me,
I, would be your father, you to look upto,
To follow in my footsteps, unconventional,
Sometimes maverick steps, sudden understanding:

A time for responsibility, to do the right thing,
Not to do the things, I'd done before,
For that was no way, for young ones to behave,
And that was no way, for a role model to act.

To be proud of you, is what I hoped,
For that to happen, there were things to change,
Ways to act, ways to teach and ways to talk,
Never believed it a walk in the park.

And with a smile, never a walk in the park,
But proud I am, you would not believe,
So proud, of you both, so young,
So beautiful, yet such impressionable ages.

I believe in you both, you make me swell,
Hold my head high, tell people we meet,
These are my sons, with broad a smile,
I know you both well, will not let me down.

Hold your heads high and meet with smiles,
Strangers, good friends, as though are all one,
No air of shyness, distance or fright,
But confidence, humour, charisma and charm.

Still at young ages, still far to go,
Let's hold what we have and improve where we can,
For love, respect and magical times,
We have had lots and lots more to come.

No better could I ask, for boys like you,
Such beauty and strength, you both hold within,
I made a promise, a promise to you both,
I looked into your eyes, at your soft, soft skin.

When You Left

Was at your side when you left,
Holding your hand and whispering in your ear,
I love you Mum, to make sure you knew.

Take these words, these words of love,
With you, be the last words you heard,
To be with you for now, forever eternal.

Beside your bed, your hospital bed,
All life stood still, while you lay there,
Waiting and hoping we'd not hear what we heard.

Ten days we waited, we stood,
We hoped, not to hear what we heard,
Time had gone on, too long, now too weak.

But those words they came,
Like a ton of molten lava,
Spreading and burning, heavy and hot.

Still now, ten years have passed,
From nowhere, like a bolt of lightning,
The grief hits, emotions they explode.

People look, I know they see,
The consumption I feel, not within,
A measure of manhood, betrayed,

Who cares what they think? Not I,
A measure of manhood, who cares?
Not I, those words they came, oh they came.

Not accepted the grief, with dignity,
Who cares? Not I, you were too young,
To go, to leave us, a life not finished.

For I know for sure, oh I know it for sure,
My sons, your grandsons, were but babes,
When your life was cut short, far too short.

Cold and Alone

Up escalators, through concourse,
From work, from shops, from life,
People trudge from benign existence,
To somewhere better they think.

I'm important, more so than you,
Face betraying a feeling, they don't know is shown,
A feeling they'd rather have kept to themselves,
Not betrayed by averting their gaze.

From solitude and cold,
To cramped and too hot,
Daily grind endured by thousands,
Millions no doubt across lands.

Into the night, to the Poetry Cafe,
Poets, performers, first night virgins,
Of which I am one, my god I am here,
Standing up front, a feeling so strange.

From age eleven, dreaded English lessons,
Snaking around class, reading page at a time,
Until, I'm up next, heart racing and pounding,
Stuttering, hating the cow, for teaching this way.

But now I do it, do it through choice,
Never would have believed it, thirty years ago,
But now through choice and belief in what I write,
What "I" write, not the words of Harper Lee.

Years passed, to use just one clichéd question,
Have I found myself? What does that mean?
Did writing, putting words down on paper,
Allow me to believe, I have something to say?

How can something so simple, so obvious,
Been staring me straight, straight in the eye,
Have been missed for so long?
Did I, did I avert my gaze?

And not allow the feelings within,
To come through and share them with you,
For something I know and I feel very sure,
We are all equal, all conceived the same way.

Off With Their Heads

Inhumane destination!
Crowded, squeezed and mushed,
The slaughterhouse,
Not Slaughterhouse 5,
Nor the one, with men,
In white coats and rubber boots.

This inhumane destination,
This inhumane journey,
Suffered daily, by the Greys,
The Suits and Media Types,
Off, to their slaughterhouses,
Or, are they, offices?

My, what a grind,
What a daily grind?
Last nights wine invading,
Too close, get away!
Bloody music too loud,
Personal invasion, space, personal space.

The slaughterhouse, or should I say, office?
Or was I right, first time?
Outcome's the same,
Off with their heads,
Out with their brains,
What a grind, that awful daily grind!

Not Explained

Words spoken, rolling off tongue to waiting ears,
Words written, quill nib to parchment paper,
Words typed, fingertips dancing on keyboard keys.

Homer not the first orator, performer,
Vibrant voice to expectant assembly,
Tales foretold again, again and again.

Generation upon next, generation,
Continued to tell and (possibly) expand,
The original tales foretold.

Every possible medium, we now have,
To record, reread and preserve,
The meaning we offer to be taken.

Meanings not explained or so we're told,
Meanings taken as written, as read,
Meanings their own to each reader.

I see this, this way, not that,
But you see that, that way, not this,
The difference the beauty of writing, of reading, of knowledge.

Beauty of writing, not explained,
Beauty of reading, not explained,
Beauty of knowledge, not explained.

The beauty, the beauty!
Of words, not explained.

Tragic Starlets

Little Em'ly, Copperfield's tragic starlet,
Betrothed to Ham, the artless fool,
Innocence stolen, ripped apart,
By Little Trot's schoolday idol.

Steerforth, guardian and protector,
Once earnest, steadfast confidante,
Turned defiler, debauched ravager,
Twenty times richer, ne'er to want.

Kemp, Larkin's alter ego'd,
Awkward, sometime imbecile,
Showed his hand to be denied,
Fair, angelic Gillian, not Jill.

Warner, Kemps forced roommate,
Ever wanting accepted equal,
Feelings, admiration, love or hate,
Classes miles apart, ne'er equal.

Common theme of innocence betrayed,
Richer by wealth but not by heart,
Em'ly, Pegotty's unworldly obligate,
Kemp, the imbecile, sycophant and puppet.

Genius

Einaudi, Metallica, Jones - Stereophonics fame,
Larkin, Dickens, Wilde - Reading Gaol fame,
Six names, six beings, not often together,
Six names, six genii, not often together.

Heroes, all heroes of mine,
Away, they take the mind,
Wonderful words, to other places,
Wonderful voices, to other faces.

If I could, could only be,
The genius within, within me?
A tiny percent, a tiny part,
Still set within, yet to d'part.

Winter Cold

Distant, like ships passing coldly,
Bows making waves, captains of vessels,
Knowing each other, not caring,
Dead now, winter cold, talking might help.

Driving through water, pushing aside,
The hell, the fire and the demons,
Hell burning inside, then freezing,
Dead now, winter cold, talking might help.

Heart encased in thin winter ice,
Blood boiling not melting away,
Why distant like ships passing coldly?
Dead now, winter cold, talking might help.

Wakes meet once vessels have passed,
One going east, one going west,
No ground in the middle to meet, thoughts cold and uncaring,
Dead now, winter cold, talking might help.

Restoration of life

Dryness in the mouth,
Quenched by one drop,
Satiated filled to bursting.

Dry sandy expanse,
Solitary desert lily,
Shimmering desert oasis.

Soul devoid of love,
One warm caring kiss,
Heart pulsating life restored.

Venture

Marianas Trench, thoughts deep and dark lie,
With the deep ocean uglies, those thoughts of despair,
A place often visited, long time ago,
No option apparent, worst feeling I've known.

When that state of mind takes over your being,
Eddies, thoughts swirling, no sense do they make,
Only one thing to do, there's nothing left,
Nothing to live for, or so it would seem.

Back from the brink, peering over the edge,
Peered into the trench, with thoughts of despair,
Thoughts swirling, no sense did they make,
When depths an abyss, with deep ocean uglies.

Counselling, put everything, into perspective,
We know we've done wrong, or so society says,
The guilt that is heaped and the burden that brings,
Once a time I would say *I have no regrets*.

No regrets I still say, for I am still here,
Still here to breathe and speak those words,
And speak them loud and teach their meaning,
To my boys and thank god I can teach them.

To regret puts a negative spin,
On the things one has ventured,
For me, I prefer to venture and fail,
And not regret but turn it to good.

Stop the ventures, fear of love, fear of life,
Curl up in a corner and lay down to die,
Sleep among the willows and the bramble bushes,
Let the frost consume your thoughts and your dreams.

Fear of life brings fear of love, three parts dead,
Bertrand Russell's immortal words,
Keep the fear from consuming the self,
Turn those three parts on their head.

Venture and fail but venture you must,
Seventy years, sometimes more, sometimes less,
But there's one thing for sure and it's deep in my thoughts,
Won't venture no more when my seventy are spent.

Last Breath

Reincarnation, no such thing,
Flesh and blood, no eternal being.

Soul? Soul? Soul?
Spiritual being?
It's all within,
Flowing crimson.

Until that crimson flows no more,
Last breath,
Cessation of life,
Draw! Draw! Please ... Draw!

Time, come and gone,
But why? Why the pain and grief?

Love is the answer,
The answer?
To everything? Good things,
Tenderness, respect, passion.

Love is the answer,
The answer?
To everything? Bad things,
Revenge, hatred, passion.

Don't hate, love, love like lovers love,
Time, is too precious.

Christmas Message

Christmas cards and fairy lights,
Christmas parties and raucous sights,
Christmas angels and silent nights.

Similar scene, this scene I guess,
Bedford to Brighton or Inverness,
The festive scene, a happy scene.

This described the festive norm,
This described the festive warm,
Here, it's happy, the festive scene.

But don't forget the unfortunate one,
Sharing the festive scene, alone,
No warmth, no comfort or company.

Share a moment, a penny or pound,
Offer that lonely soul, *Come round,*
Join in the joy, the company.

Might get knocked back or *bugger off!*
Might come round and scoff, scoff, scoff,
Be happy within, you've made the offer.

You never know, he might be wise,
He might be a bugger and tell terrible lies,
but you'll never know, unless you offer.

Sun Worshippers

Naked branches, left to right, back and fore,
swaying, just the remnants of last years growth
sitting, waiting dormant 'til buds spring forth,
bursting through it's crust the new year's oath

to grow again. New leaves year on year,
never failing, never dallying in their efforts,
to please the view, fill the optic sphere
with nature's beauty. Each leaf affords

a beauty bestowed by all things light
and airy, repaying the debt during hours
of Summer Sun. Longer days; respite
from the cold, Spring to life, flowers

aplenty, now high up above a once,
not so long ago, darkened horizon,
bringer of life and floral brilliance.
Ages have worshipped, life bringer, our Sun.

Autumn Boughs

Laying beneath the autumn boughs,
Beyond, the clear crisp blue sky,
Children swinging back and fore,
Like the sea upon the shore.

Gran and Gramps, the tidal energy,
The energy of eternal ebb and flow,
Pushing prams the doting eyes, afore,
Now time to spend, whence none before.

Sunday Afternoon, Last Sun

Some sit they chat,
About the week's events,
Others sit and watch,
Survey today's tidings.

These times so few,
Of chill and relaxation,
So varied options,
From not so long ago.

Crowds gather to enjoy the Sun,
The last Sun of this year's wet months,
Grab what they can, before it darkens,
Leaves abandoning their branches to mulch.

Sunday afternoons, times gone by,
Once a home-bound time,
Families full of mothers labours,
To satisfy the week's missed togetherness.

Now options aplenty,
Of things to do,
Of time to spend together,
Are these more gathered times?

The Sun has Come Out

Finally, finally, the Sun has come out,
Early morning birdsong, buds opening,
Beginning to open, like a huge weight lifted,
From shoulders so heavy, not now.

The long, dark and dreary days,
Like a distant memory,
How the mood changes,
With early morning, birdsong.

Birdsong lasting, morning to dusk,
Lifting the weight of winter bleakness.
Take it away, like fog lifting and spreading,
A fog of miserable winter darkness.

Open the door, for Spring to spring forth,
Cut grass and Spring's first daffodils,
The beauty, relief, these things bring,
Taking away that winter bleakness.

Finally, finally, the Sun has come out.

Insomnia

Tossing and turning 'til I take no more,
Dog disturbed by the creaking door,
Kettle loud like 2am drummer,
Live cricket from down under.

Searching twitter and irrelevant blogs,
It's all turned into a disturbing smog,
Another coffee and another smoke,
All lights out, a nocturnal cloak.

Incessant comments on the bowler's arm,
Adverts aimed at blokey charm,
Kiwis smashing that heavy hard ball,
The Pakistani total far too small.

Far too awake to contemplate sleep,
Lay and toss, those bloody sheep,
Adverts again, shoot 'em up movie,
Vorsprung durch Technik, tough and moody.

Voices

auditurus esse insolitus vox vocis

They're in my head, the noises,
There in my head, the voices.
Screeching, screaming, noises, voices.

Naughty Boys' Driving Class

A gale force wind with pigeons thrashing,
Into fallen trees, careless drivers crashing,
Pigeons roosting amid hedges and thicket,
Call off the Sunday afternoon cricket.

There'll be no third man or silly mid off,
No bragging in clubhouse from banking toff,
That toff who's car swerved then went crashing,
On his way to the wicket, with hopes of smashing,

That little red ball over mid wicket,
And knock the pigeon, out of the thicket,
Then try to explain why he drove so fast,
Before being offered, a *naughty boys' driving class*.

Empty Page

Empty page, empty page,
Sing to me, sing to me.

Don't leave me here,
With nothing to write.

Give me something,
Something to write.

Something other,
Other than white.

Don't go !
Don't leave !

Come back !
Empty page, don't leave.

You've left,
You're gone.

Empty page,
You're gone.

Urban Fox

Cold creeps through the open door,
Penetrating bone,
Dark obscurest scene,
What lurks within that darkness?

Branches rustle, softest movement,
Alarms betraying silence,
Windows reflecting from within,
What is that moving out there?

Slightest breeze awakens stillness,
The stillness of the night,
Dark descended hours ago,
I'm sure there's something out there.

They look like stars within the bed,
Something moved I saw for sure,
Eyes reflect the dimmest bulb,
I've not gone mad, it was there.

STOPPED dead still and then a scamper,
Swiftness leaving just a blur,
Man's eyes no time to adjust,
Night prowl of the urban fox ... I think.

Migrant Blackbird

The wild flurry of the new autumn Blackbird,
As a threat to avoid, it has seen, or heard,
A warning to others of what's been seen, or heard,
The flurry and scamper to somewhere safe.

A wild flurry betraying possibilities,
A song so sweet and tuneful,
Mesmerising if only a minute or more,
Spent allowing it's penetration, into the mind.

The new autumn migrants,
Nervy and scared, new surroundings,
Long distance on the wing to reach these shores,
Our gardens, our fields and our woods.

I wonder is this a transit stop,
A place to feed and gain strength,
Or will this, my garden, my piece of suburbia,
Be your resting place, your playhouse, your auditorium?

An abundance of fruit and of berries,
Lie waiting for you and your flock,
To arrive and feast to your hearts content,
On unloved and abandoned fruit trees.

Trees that have stood and forced fruit,
For many years, they have flourished,
Now untethered, unloved and untended,
In the old ladies' garden, no longer a treat,

But a burden in later life now housebound,
A time gone by when gathered and shared,
With friends and family, too many to use,
For now, unable, to open the door, let alone gather fruit.

Flown in from far afield, from northern climes,
Where the snow has started it's winter onslaught,
While the weather was mellow and southwesterlies prevailed,
Until winter set in and daylight hours dwindled.

When the days become longer and life bounds afresh,
The sun lifting higher above trees, hills and buildings,
Not the quick winter scurry just peeking it's glare,
Above rain covered roads, waiting to blind.

Spring will send the migrants back,
Back to sing, penetrate minds on distant shores,
With the mesmerising song, a minute or more,
Spent listening intently until the scared scamper,

Takes you away from moments of peace,
Shared so willingly with you, our yellow beaked friend,
Can listen to the melodious tune you share,
From Autumn through Spring, eternity wished.

The migrants all gone just the faithful remain,
The native Blackbird, suburban corner we share,
So willingly, just for the moments of peace,
Shattered by song, so melodious and sweet.

Red Breast

The tick tick tick
Of the red-breasted Robin,
Followed by it's
Melodious evensong:
Foretelling of territory,
Gained, to be kept:
Song attracting mates,
At the onset of,
Breeding season.

Fallen Oak

Needles pricking into the face,
The vast expanse and open space,
The needles driving, bare skinned
Face, exposed to the rain and wind.

The frozen hoof print, ready to catch
You out, the print not much of a match,
For the boots are sturdy, they're strong,
The pace to keep against the throng,

The onslaught, contempt, wave after wave,
The storm keeps hitting, battering the slave
Of winter, walk and walk, blood pumping,
Up and down hills, legs and lungs screaming.

The dismal scene from months gone
By, uprooted Oak, roots exposed, bygone
Times the Royal has stood and fought,
The wind, the rain, the final onslaught.

The gales and gusts the final act,
The path we've walked along and tracked
Many times before: just firewood, embers and smoke,
the future now, for that exposed, bygoned, Royal Oak.

Embryo

Beginnings of life,
Strength harnessed,
Like the daffodil bulb,
Just planted,
Energy stored,
Then consumed,
Blossom, beauty,
Bursting through.

Coffee and Croissants

Let's go now, decision made in a flash,
Before the rain comes down, splash splash,
Quick, quick, don't muse and don't dawdle,
We'll be home for coffee and croissants.

Rush, rush and down came the tent,
Away went the surfboards, money all spent,
Quick, quick, pack away and don't dawdle,
We'll be home for coffee and croissants.

So drove through the night, oh the deafening snores,
From front and back, that would knock down doors,
Quick, quick, don't stop and don't dawdle,
We'll be home for coffee and croissants.

Drowsy, what a morning, torrential downpour,
After grabbing a couple of hours, no more,
Quick, quick, I slept, no didn't dawdle,
Thank god for coffee and croissants.

Layman's Creed and All That

I've done time, not that type of time,
Done time, stood up and assembled,
We believe in one God, the Father, the Almighty,
maker of Heaven and Earth, the Nicene Creed and all that.

I,
Little old me,
Prefer to believe, in a good Man,
Many men but this Man,
Iesus Nazarenus Rex Iudaeorum.

Spoke out for what he believed,
Beliefs, not conventional or - right,
Be careful His friends whispered,
Stood by Him, til the last, most.

Tracked down, captured, humiliated,
Tortured, nailed, left to die,
One to His right, one to His Left,
Jesus the Nazarene King of the Jews.

Nailed, through hands, nailed through feet,
Nailed, suppos'd friend, suppos'd follower,
Last thoughts, of forgiveness,
For the nailers and the nailer.

Forgiveness, a wonderful gift,
Wonderful ability and state,
Of the mind, to forgive and offer prayers,
When nailed, crucified and dying.

Might still be there if these were the words,
When stood up and assembled,
I believe in one Jesus, the Man, the Forgiver,
maker of Christianity and Faith, the Layman's Creed and all that.

I See the Stars

I see the stars,
I feel the cold,
Is that one Mars?
I must behold!

I hope it is,
I hope it is,
No star but Mars,
It must be Mars.

It can't be Mars,
They are all stars,
We can't see Mars,
Behind the bars.

When I am free,
I'll go to Mars,
If I could see,
Not only stars.

Today, I'm Within

Today, I'm within, not with-out,
You must, be polite, be pleasant,
But why, why bother?
Not today, leave me alone.

Contemplating (being grumpy),
Today, not a day,
For talking, laughing and joking,
Today, a day in, within, myself.

Why? Don't know,
Don't have that answer,
Position of the moon, the stars and sky?
Don't know.

Later today, tomorrow, later still,
Will open my soul and mouth,
Bright smile and jovial,
'Til then, I'll be contemplating (being grumpy).

Won't apologise, won't shout or fight,
It just happens, that answer?
Space today, please, some space,
In time, will stop contemplating (being grumpy).

My Message

Light atop, dark below,
Floating like ghosts,
Breaking and changing,
Clear form, now ragged, still drifting.

Faster today, leaves rustle more vibrant,
Odd sparkle of Sun,
Warmth on the skin, warmth within,
Whitewash dazzling.

Drifting, west to east,
Drifting, no purpose or plan,
Drifting, coast to coast,
Drifting, day to day.

A break in the Cumulus,
Cirrus up high,
Like a message foretelling the future,
Future, where lies my message?

Driven off the Road

Driven off the road, or so it would seem,
For no other reason she could fathom,
She'd ended up, car smashed to smithereens,
In the ditch from which she now climbed.

The rain was driving, into her face, feet slipping,
The now mud, just hours before, firm embankment.
She remembered a flash, flash of blinding light,
How long had she been unconscious?

Her head now pounding, not just rain running down
Her face: the crimson tinge mingled with rain
The pumping in her head increasing. *How long
Have I been asleep?* Her watch had stopped, no idea

Where her phone had gone. She kept on up the slope
Until she saw headlights, waving her arms for help,
She saw the car slow down. Then without a hint
Of remorse, the damaged car sped up and hit her.

Flew her flying, through the air, the last thing that
Flew through her mind, the last thing that she saw,
The brother, the bastard savage rapist,
She'd not seen since she went to the cops.

www.ingramcontent.com/pod-product-compliance
Lightning Source LLC
Chambersburg PA
CBHW071739020426
42331CB00008B/2101